hRya

SPACE
SYSTEMS

Telescopes, Probes, Spacecraft, and the Future of Space Exploration

Elizabeth Schmermund

Cavendish
Square
New York

Library of Congress Cataloging-in-Publication Data

Names: Schmermund, Elizabeth.
Title: Telescopes, probes, spacecraft, and the future of space exploration / Elizabeth Schmermund.
Description: New York : Cavendish Square Publishing, 2017. | Series: Space systems | Includes index.
Identifiers: ISBN 9781502622938 (library bound) | ISBN 9781502622945 (ebook)
Subjects: LCSH: Outer space--Exploration--Juvenile literature. | Outer space--Exploration--Technological innovations--Juvenile literature.
Classification: LCC QB500.22 S34 2017 | DDC 520--dc23

Editorial Director: David McNamara
Editor: Caitlyn Miller
Copy Editor: Rebecca Rohan
Associate Art Director: Amy Greenan
Senior Designer: Alan Sliwinski
Production Coordinator: Karol Szymczuk
Photo Research: J8 Media

Contents

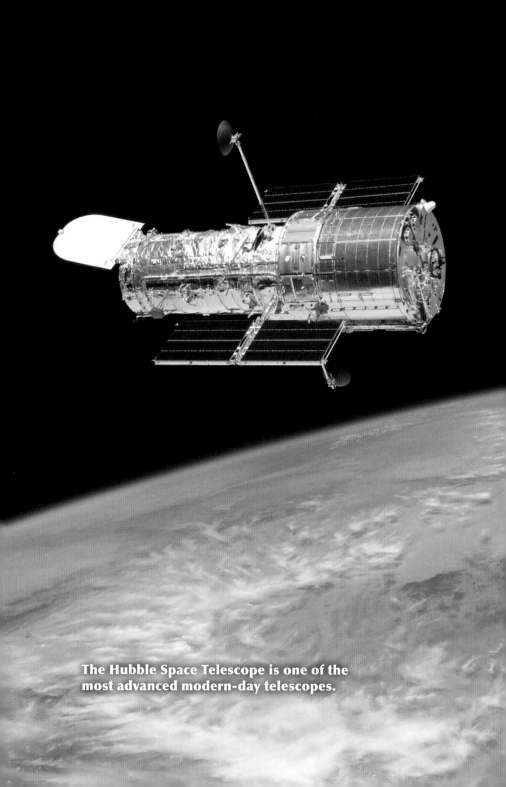

The Hubble Space Telescope is one of the most advanced modern-day telescopes.

Introduction:
The Evolution of
Space Technology

Some of the earliest inventions ever made by humans
were machines to make looking at the sky easier. While
certainly not as old as the wheel, rudimentary lenses were
first developed over two thousand years ago. These lenses
were made with **concave** mirrors and water; according
to some ancient sources, they were made for the express
purpose of bending the sun's rays. (Of course, at that time,
people were unaware of the physical laws that govern optics
and the properties of light.) The astrolabe, considered by
many to be the greatest invention of the ancient world, was
an astronomical computer that could tell and predict the
positions of the sun, moon, planets, and stars in the night
sky. These inventions were the beginning of humankind's
development to explore the cosmos.

While there is no consensus as to who invented the telescope, it was generally agreed to have been developed in the sixteenth century. During this time, developments in glassmaking allowed glassworkers to grind lenses with more precision. According to science writer Lauren Cox, "In the late 1500s, someone held up two lenses and discovered what they could do."

What they could do, of course, was make very distant objects appear incredibly close, allowing a viewer to discern details on the surface of the object that would never have been perceived before. This would become the greatest invention of the Scientific Revolution in the seventeenth century, when many people, curious to observe and ask and attempt to solve questions about the world around them, provided the basis for what we now call the scientific method—and modern science. In 1608, a Dutch eyeglass maker named Hans Lippershey applied for a patent for a telescope that could magnify objects three times their actual size. The race for greater inventions to access the cosmos was on.

Today, of course, we no longer need to access space from Earth—we can go there ourselves. The development of the American space program, the race to launch the first **satellites**, and the race to the moon all pushed humankind further than ever before. No longer must we be content to observe the sky through lenses—although our telescopes are now incredibly powerful machines that can observe the distant cosmos or are launched into orbit themselves, like the famous Hubble Space Telescope. Since the 1960s, astronomers have been sent into space—at first in technologically limited spacecraft and at great personal risk to themselves. Now, there is an almost continual presence on the International Space Station (ISS), a man-made habitable satellite and one of the most advanced machines humankind has ever built.

The ISS and other satellites are held in Earth's orbit by the force of gravity, which is also what holds together all the celestial bodies in our Milky Way galaxy and the larger universe, and causes some celestial bodies, like Earth and other planets, to orbit around larger objects, like the sun. By using the physical laws that govern our universe to humankind's advantage in space exploration, we have developed technologies that have propelled us away from Earth, deeper into the stars. We have orbited (and landed on) the moon, and have send satellites to the far reaches of our solar system. The Hubble Telescope, which itself is in orbit around the Earth, allows us to see star systems millions of light years away from us.

But scientists plan to go far beyond just observing other planets and stars. Private companies such as SpaceX, owned by well-known entrepreneur Elon Musk, have developed new technologies, such as rockets that can land back on Earth and be reused for future missions. Many of these companies are also at the forefront of plans to send regular people into space and, like the Mars One project, to eventually colonize Mars. Private companies are not the only ones at the forefront of this exciting and ambitious plan. In 2016, the National Aeronautics and Space Administration (NASA) publicized its plans to establish permanent human settlements on Mars by 2030. Comparing this journey to the early settlement of the United States, NASA claims that what we once thought of as science fiction or fantasy will soon be a reality. Our understanding of the universe through new technologies is rapidly changing, and we are living through an important moment in this development. We are also at the threshold of an entirely new period for humanity—one in which we may no longer be dependent on Earth, and may become part of the more distant cosmos ourselves.

To some, all of this may sound far-fetched. Many scientists have voiced concern over these plans, stating that, based on both current funding and current technologies, these goals will not be met anytime soon. On the other hand, space technologies are developing at an increasingly rapid pace. Who knows how these new technologies will change our lives—and our ambitions—in the next ten years?

Once, long ago, a revolution occurred when Galileo Galilei looked through his early telescope and determined, based on his observations, that Earth must be revolving around the sun. (Galileo's observations confirmed Nicolaus Copernicus's theory that the solar system was **heliocentric**.) Another revolution guided by the use of space technology occurred when the first artificial satellite, called *Sputnik 1*, was launched in 1957 by the Soviet Union. Many more subsequent revolutions in astronomical understanding have followed. But we live in a particularly exciting time today. In the past ten years, astronomers and astrophysicists have discovered more planets than ever before, revised our knowledge of the planets in our solar system, and determined that our universe is not only expanding, but also accelerating. None of this would have been possible without the technological tools that scientists and inventors have developed in response to our continual quest for knowledge about our universe.

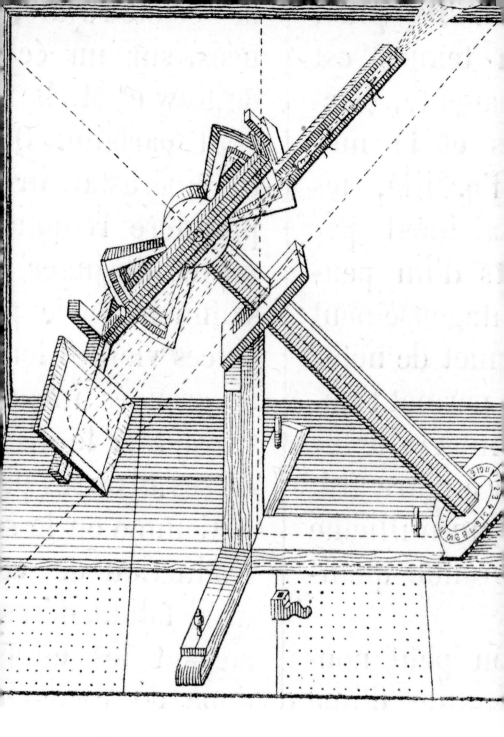

Galileo's first telescope revolutionized observational astronomy.

Early Inventions

S imple lenses have been around for thousands of years, practically since the dawn of human civilization. Early Greek and Arabic philosophers wrote treatises about **refracting** and **reflecting** light. These early investigations laid the groundwork for the most important technological invention for observational astronomy: the telescope.

The use of the telescope was imperative to better understanding our universe because of the enormity of what we were trying to see. There are approximately one hundred billion galaxies in the universe. In our galaxy, the Milky Way, there are approximately three hundred billion stars. Our solar system, which describes the planets that revolve around our star, the sun, is itself very large. For example, if Earth were the size of a classroom globe, the moon would be the size of a baseball orbiting Earth from approximately

40 feet (12.1 meters) away. However, the sun would be a sphere approximately fourteen stories tall and located about 3 miles (4.8 kilometers) away. Neptune, which would stand about 5 feet (1.5 m) tall in this model, would be nearly 90 miles (149 km) away. Astronomical distances are almost unfathomably large and, without the help of powerful telescopes, our understanding of the universe would be limited to the objects we can see with the naked eye.

EARLY TELESCOPES

In the late 1500s and early 1600s, many factors came together to enable inquisitive minds to develop the telescope. About 150 years earlier, eyeglasses had become more advanced, allowing both nearsightedness and farsightedness to be corrected using both concave and **convex** lenses. Although eyeglasses used for reading texts and seeing right in front of your nose might seem very different from the development of telescopes that allow us to peer into the dark recesses of the universe, they are actually very similar and based on the same optical principles. In fact, it was an eyeglass maker, Hans Lippershey, who first applied for a patent for a telescope in 1608. This telescope could magnify an object by three times its actual size. Lippershey used both a concave eyepiece and a convex lens in his invention. Scholars today are not sure if he was the first one to have actually thought to pair these innovations to develop a telescope, but he was the first to apply for a patent and, thus, the first to receive credit. Many assume today that this may have been common knowledge among eyeglass makers or, at least, other eyeglass makers knew of this phenomenon, although they may not have thought of its practical application.

Like many inventions, the telescope would not prove its full utility until it fell into the right hands. Those would be the hands of Galileo Galilei, the famous Italian astronomer. In 1609, less than one year after Lippershey applied for his patent, Galileo was in Venice when he heard news of the invention from intellectual circles there. Although he had little knowledge of how Lippershey had built his telescope, Galileo knew enough about optics and physics to plan out the construction of his own telescope, then called a "perspective glass," by the time he arrived back home in Padua. Using a tube made of lead, he fixed a convex lens on one side of the tube and a convex lens on the other side. He worked with his design until he had an improved and workable telescope. Returning to Venice a few days later, he disclosed his new invention to the Venetian public and to the Senate—earning instant fame and a larger salary at the University of Padua.

But Galileo's telescope was not just for prestige and financial gain. He also wanted to use his telescope to observe the stars. Galileo spent the next year improving his design, then directed it at the satellites of Jupiter in 1610, discovering that the planet had a group of moons that orbited around it.

What Is the Difference between Reflection and Refraction?

Telescopes depend on either reflection or refraction to operate. Reflection is what happens to light when it bounces off a mirror and returns back to the viewer. Refraction occurs when light passes through a medium, like glass for example, and bends as it does so.

A refractor telescope, the earliest kind of telescope, uses two lenses to bend light toward the eye of the viewer. Such a telescope could also use a mirror to help direct the light down the central tube.

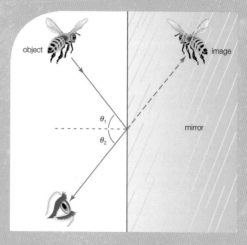

This diagram illustrates the law of reflection, used in reflector telescopes.

The mirror might focus and direct the light, but it does not magnify the image. Rather, it is the eyepiece that does so. This is typically what many people think of when they think of a standard telescope.

A reflector telescope, however, depends more on mirrors. Light is not routed directly to the viewer's eye, but is rather bounced from one mirror at the bottom of the telescope to another secondary mirror, which then bounces the light off the eyepiece. The eyepiece lens is what magnifies the light as it is directed to the viewer's eye. The benefit of having many mirrors is that you can have a shorter tube. As the light bounces back and forth, it will travel as far as it would have with a longer tube, standard on a refractor telescope for example, but in a shorter amount of space. Today, reflector telescopes are the most advanced kinds of telescopes.

The most important discovery that Galileo would make was something that another astronomer had theorized before him. In the early 1500s, Nicolaus Copernicus, a mathematician and astronomer, published *De revolutionibus*, an influential text that stated that, rather than a geocentric model where Earth was the center of the solar system, our solar system was based on a heliocentric model in which planets, including Earth, revolved around the sun. This model was considered by many to be not just wrong, but heretical. If Earth was not the center of the known universe, it would appear as if humankind did not hold a special place in the universe after all. To the Catholic Church, this was wrong—and dangerous to their teachings. Copernicus died shortly after this text was published and, with the author not around to defend it, the scientific community largely rejected it. That is, until Galileo turned his telescope up to the sky.

The definitive proof that the sun sits at the center of our solar system came not from Galileo's observations of the sun, but his observations of the phases of Venus. To the human eye, Venus always appears the same in the night sky. However, with the help of Galileo's telescope, the astronomer was able to observe how the planet was partially in darkness in specific patterns throughout a period of time. Galileo knew that these phases were caused by the planet's movement around the sun; there was no other reason why Venus would be shrouded in darkness at various times. This was the evidence Galileo needed to prove that the heliocentric model of our solar system was indeed correct. Although it took some convincing (Galileo famously refused to recant his belief in the heliocentric model before Catholic inquisition, and was placed under house arrest for the remainder of his life), the heliocentric model was proved true beyond a doubt in the eighteenth and nineteenth centuries. None of this would have been possible if Galileo hadn't affixed two lenses to the end of a leaden tube, pointed it to the night sky, and changed the course of history.

FURTHER REFINEMENTS OF THE TELESCOPE

After Galileo's original design, many others in the scientific community began to experiment with making their own telescopes. The famous astronomer Johannes Kepler included designs for a more complex telescope, composed of two convex lenses, in a 1611 book. While Kepler is not known to have constructed the telescope himself, his book provided the blueprint for subsequent astronomers to construct these kinds of telescopes. By the 1700s, Kepler's telescope became more popular than Galileo's telescope. This was because Kepler's telescope, with two convex lenses, offered a larger field of vision when observing the sky.

Further refinements were made during this century by lengthening the objective lens, which provided longer focal lengths, thus providing a sharper image for astronomers. However, lengthening telescopes made them heavier and harder to hold up. Oftentimes, slight changes in the air would cause the long tube of the telescope to vibrate, making it difficult to see anything. While changes were being made to telescopes, they had a long way to go.

Isaac Newton, the famous physicist, made other important contributions to the telescope. In 1668, he used established knowledge about curved mirrors that act like lenses to build the world's first reflecting telescope. Today called a "Newtonian telescope," this early reflecting telescope used a concave primary mirror in conjunction with a flat diagonal secondary mirror. These telescopes were easy to make for an amateur (making it popular still with amateur astronomers today), had a wide field of view, and exhibited no **chromatic aberration**, commonly found in the earlier refracting telescopes, which made it difficult to see images clearly. (In the eighteenth century, John Dollond would invent achromatic lenses to decrease this optical problem with refracting telescopes.) However, the Newtonian telescope was also limited in that objects could be distorted and the secondary mirror could get in the field of view, sometimes obstructing what the astronomer wanted to see in the first place! Various astronomers, after Newton introduced his telescope, worked to refine the reflecting telescope, including John Hadley and Laurent Cassegrain.

Astronomer William Herschel's 40-foot (12 m) telescope, built in 1774, was the largest telescope ever built at the time.

However, in 1774, William Herschel made the greatest advancement in current telescope technology when he created a 40-foot (12 m) reflecting telescope, the largest telescope ever made until that point. He removed the diagonal secondary mirror to cut down on any obstruction in the field of view and tilted the primary mirror in such a way as to view the object directly. Known as the Herschelian telescope, he was able to discover a new Saturnine moon the first night he pointed it to the sky. Herschel's design remained the largest telescope for fifty years, and his telescope became immensely popular. However, there was a major drawback to such reflecting telescopes: due to the nature of the metal mirrors, they would have to be removed monthly and repolished to continue to work efficiently. Not only was this a tremendous amount of work, but every time the mirror was polished, it would need to be refigured (reshaped) before being placed back on the telescope.

Largely due to this problem, refracting telescopes remained more popular than reflecting telescopes throughout the 1800s. But refracting telescopes had their own limitations: they grew larger and larger, making it more difficult to construct such large lenses with precision. The tables turned once again. At the beginning of the twentieth century, technological developments that allowed scientists to deposit a layer of silver on telescope mirrors caused reflecting telescopes to once again take the lead. This solved the problem that had caused reflecting telescopes to lose popularity among the astronomy community. By 1917, two large, modern, reflecting telescopes were built that would change the course of astronomy: the 60-inch (152-centimeter) Hale telescope and the 100-inch (254 cm) Hooker telescope. Both of these telescopes were located at Mount Wilson Observatory outside of Los Angeles, California, where the high altitude and clear skies of the area could be used to astronomers' advantage. Another technological development occurred when the silver lining was replaced with longer-lasting aluminum lining. This meant that the mirrors could go longer periods of time without having their lining replaced. These two telescopes would be beaten, in size at least, by the construction of the 200-inch (5.1 m) Hale reflecting telescope in 1948 at Mount Palomar, in San Diego, California. The era of our modern telescopes had begun.

SPACE PROBES

Humankind was not content to just remain on earth and point telescopes up at the night sky. On October 4, 1957, humankind's relationship with space changed forever when the Soviet Union launched the first artificial satellite into orbit. This satellite was called *Sputnik 1* and was about the size of a beach ball, weighing less than 200 pounds (91 kilograms). Four radio antennae erupted from the metal sphere, allowing the satellite to send radio pulses that were detectable on Earth. Although *Sputnik 1* did not have sensors, it was still an important scientific experiment. Soviet scientists were able to study how such an object interacted in low earth orbit, and they were also able to study the upper atmosphere by the speed loss the satellite incurred in orbit. Anyone who looked up in the sky during a certain period of time would be able to see *Sputnik* orbiting the Earth.

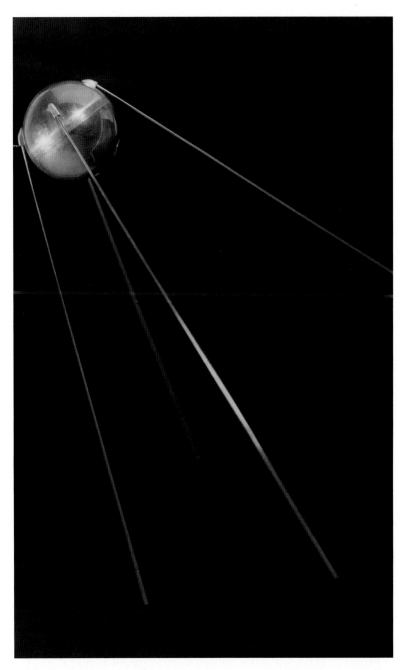

The launch of *Sputnik I* took Americans by surprise and began the frantic "space race" between the United States and the Soviet Union.

Sputnik 1 spent three months in orbit before burning up upon reentering the Earth's atmosphere in January 1958.

Perhaps the most important effect of *Sputnik* was a political one. The United States, embroiled in the Cold War with the Soviet Union, was unaware that their rivals had the technology to launch a satellite into space. Many scholars state that US President Eisenhower was aware of the Soviets' technology, but that American politicians and the American public at large led the public outcry that the United States was technologically lagging behind their Cold War enemy. Worried that Soviet technology surpassed their own (not just, of course, in astronomical research, but also for military purposes), the United States ramped up its program to not only launch its own artificial satellite, but to send the first astronauts into outer space. Thus, the Space Race began.

Soon after the launch of *Sputnik 1*, the United States developed its own successful satellites, including *Explorer 1*, *Project SCORE*, and *Courier 1B*. *Explorer 1* was the first US satellite ever when it was launched on January 31, 1958. This satellite was much smaller than *Sputnik 1*, weighing in at only about 30 pounds (13.6 kg), and was able to return basic data back to mission control until its batteries died in orbit four months later.

With the creation of the Advanced Research Projects Agency (ARPA) in 1958, more developments in space technology were made. President Eisenhower formed ARPA largely as a response to *Sputnik 1*, and the agency was meant to research and develop new technology to "expand the frontiers of space." The first ARPA project, *Project SCORE*, was launched on December 18, 1958, from the *Atlas* rocket. This was an important step in space technology because the *Atlas* rocket was 100 times larger than any previous US satellite. Just as importantly, the first transmission from space came from *Project SCORE*, when President Eisenhower broadcast a previously recorded Christmas message via shortwave radio from a tape recorder aboard the satellite.

Another important—and more famous—agency was developed in 1958 in response to the Soviet's *Sputnik 1*. On July 29, 1958, President Eisenhower signed the National Aeronautics and Space Act. This act established the National Aeronautics and Space Administration (NASA) as an independent agency of the federal government focused on aeronautics research and developing the space program. Previously existing agencies were incorporated into NASA, including the earlier National Advisory Committee for Aeronautics (NACA). NASA's main task moving forward was manned spaceflight. They wanted to send a rocket ship into space that would carry astronauts. One of the first projects that NASA worked on was called X-15. This top-secret project used a hypersonic rocket ship operated by the US Air Force. Nearly two hundred flights were launched as part of this project, piloted by specially selected Air Force pilots. The flights succeeded in reaching the frontier of the Earth's atmosphere and outer space and proved to be vital early experiments in the Space Race. In fact, two of the flights succeeded in reaching the Air Force's definition of outer space by reaching an altitude of over fifty miles above earth. These pilots were technically the first astronauts.

Just as the United States was experimenting with sending men into space, so, too, was the Soviet Union conducting its own experiments. Shortly after the *Sputnik 1* launch, *Sputnik 2* was launched. This time, however, the Soviets had placed a dog, named Laika, in the satellite. They wanted to test what happened to an animal in outer space, knowing that the dog would not survive the journey. Laika died about five hours into the flight from overheating when the heat control was not properly regulated. (A monument for Laika was built in 2008 and stands near the Moscow building where her flight was planned.)

SPACECRAFT

Of course, all of these early space probes and artificial satellites were only the beginning of the Space Race—and practice for the real event. For both Americans and the Soviets, the real test of who won the Space Race was sending an astronaut up to space—and returning the astronaut safely back to Earth.

In 1961, the Soviet Union again stunned America and the world with the launch of the first manned spacecraft, called the *Vostok 1*. The astronaut, Yuri Gagarin, completed a single orbit around the Earth and became the first human to cross into outer space. The bravery of these early astronauts, or cosmonauts as they were commonly called, cannot be underestimated; at this point in time, the Soviet Union had only a 50 percent success rate with its rocket launches. And no one knew exactly what would happen once Gagarin reached outer space—or how he would return safely back to Earth. The *Vostok 1* spent about an hour in orbit before commands were sent to the reentry module. From this tiny, metal cylinder, Gagarin fell back to Earth, supported by parachutes. After this momentous voyage, Gagarin would joke about how he landed near a farmer, exited from the module, and said, "[D]on't be afraid, I am a Soviet citizen like you, who has descended from space and I must find a telephone to call Moscow!"

The Soviet farmer must have been incredulous; but what appeared to be science fiction was actually fast becoming a reality.

The Mauna Kea Observatory,
located on the Big Island of Hawaii

The Modern Understanding of Space Technology

2

Telescopes, probes, and spacecraft have come a long way
since those early days. Today, telescopes are enormous
machines, which can be connected to a network of telescopes
both on Earth and in satellite and can detect a wide range
of wavelengths. Spacecraft are no longer small metal balls
that can hold one astronaut; they are incredibly complex
inventions that can not only send astronauts into outer space
and bring them home safely, but sustain life for extended
periods of time in outer space (like, for example, the
International Space Station).

OPTICAL TELESCOPES

Today, most professional astronomers use refractor telescopes,
not reflector telescopes. One reason for this, as discussed
in the last chapter, is because reflector telescopes can be

made very large and do not have the size limitations of refraction telescopes. In addition, refractor telescopes are cheaper to make and do not have chromatic aberration. For a large portion of the twentieth century, there was not much technological development with ground telescopes after they reached a certain size. Technology had to wait until the early 1990s, when the development of more advanced space-based technology allowed space telescopes to be built.

For a long time, the 200-inch (5.1 m) Hale Telescope at Palomar Observatory, which began construction in 1936 and was completed in 1948, was the largest and most advanced ground-based telescope in the world. One of the reasons why the Hale Telescope took almost ten years to construct was because of the complex engineering required to build its mirror. The mirror was one of the first major projects to use Pyrex glass, which does not expand like regular glass when heated (thus making it a favorite for kitchenware, as well!). Using Pyrex, Hale engineers understood, would prevent the mirror from changing shape even slightly, thus preventing distortion of the image. Instead of using one large mold to create the mirror, engineers used thirty-six molds that were then fused together, creating a honeycomb pattern. This was done to create multiple mounting points so that the weight of the mirror could be distributed evenly. During the first pouring of the molten Pyrex glass into the molds, the extreme heat caused the metal molds to break their bonds. This was

For many years, the 200-inch (508 cm) Hale Telescope at Palomar Observatory was the largest telescope in the world.

an expensive and time-consuming error, and engineers had to rebuild the mold. After the mold cooled (a period which took several months), the large mirror was transported via train from New York to California, where a Caltech team refined the shape of the mirror so that it was perfectly concave. Finally, the aluminum layer was deposited to prevent having to repolish the mirror.

When the 200-inch (5.1 m) Hale Telescope opened in 1948, scientists noticed that there were some distortions to the images the telescope captured. Corrections to the telescope, thus, continued until 1949, when it opened for research. It has been in operation ever since, along with the older 60-inch (1.5 m) Hale Telescope. Today, additional adjustments have been made to the telescope to outfit it with newer technologies, such as **spectrographs**, and adaptive optics. Adaptive optics is an important technology, first developed in the mid-twentieth century, whereby small adjustments are made to so-called "deformable" mirrors in order to correct any image distortions. Working in conjunction with adaptive optics, lucky imaging is another newer form of technology that has been retroactively added to the Hale Telescope. Following research done at Caltech and Cambridge University in 2007, astronomers outfitted the telescope with a high-speed camera with short **exposure** times. This allows astronomers to observe very small changes in the Earth's atmosphere. Selecting only exposures that show minimal atmospheric shifts (only 10 percent of these exposures can be selected, giving the name to "lucky imaging"), these images are combined into a single image that provides a much higher resolution than longer exposure images do. Together with adaptive optics, this has pushed the telescope's resolution to its current technological limit.

KECK TELESCOPES

The Keck I Telescope in Mauna Kea, on the Big Island of Hawaii, beat the 200-inch (5.1 m) Hale Telescope (and the BTA-6 telescope in Russia, built in 1975) to become the largest optical telescope in the world in 1993. Three years later, in 1996, the second Keck Telescope (Keck II) was built next to it. Construction on the first Keck Telescope began in 1985, with a $70 million grant from American businessman Howard B. Keck. At nearly 400 inches (10.2 m), this telescope could only be created through new technological developments that allowed engineers to operate many smaller mirrors as a single, large mirror through computer control. This had many benefits, including lifting the previous size restraint that could distort optics due to the pressure from very large (and very heavy) mirrors. The materials used to make the mirror had also come a long way, technologically speaking. Rather than using Pyrex, as engineers did on the 200-inch (5.1 m) Hale Telescope, Keck engineers used Zerodur, a glass-ceramic with a very low coefficient of thermal expansion, meaning that the material does not change shape in extreme temperatures. (This makes it particularly useful to create space telescopes, where other materials can be distorted in the extremely cold environment of outer space.) The total weight of each telescope is more than 300 tons (272 metric tons).

Although the Keck Telescopes have been surpassed in size by the 10.4 m (410 in) Gran Telescopio Canarias, or Great Canary Telescope, in Spain, constructed in 2007, they remain the most used and most productive telescopes in the world. Like Hale, the Keck telescopes have been retrofitted with the newest technology, including high-tech cameras and spectrographs that allow it to see across the visible and near **infrared** spectrums, as well as laser guide star adaptive optics. However, it's not just the instrumentation that makes the Keck Telescopes so powerful—it's the site. Located at one of the highest points in the world, the summit of Mauna Kea where the telescopes are located stands 13,766 feet (4,196 m) above the Pacific Ocean. Mauna Kea is an active volcano and there are no other mountains around to disturb the upper atmosphere. In addition to this, the island is sparsely populated, and there are no large cities around, reducing any light pollution. Finally, the weather in this part of Hawaii is typically calm, warm, and dry, allowing for better observation. The only issue, however, is the altitude. Astronomers have to become acclimated to the high-altitude site, lest they experience altitude sickness. The observatory even comes equipped with oxygen tanks for researchers who have fainted or are feeling light-headed due to lack of oxygen in the thin high-altitude atmosphere!

RADIO TELESCOPES

Since Galileo's time, telescopes have become a wide range of inventions used to observe the sky in different ways. Optical

The Arecibo Radio Telescope in Puerto Rico is the second-largest dish antenna in the world.

telescopes, such as the refractor telescopes described above, are only a portion of telescopes in use today. There are also many radio telescopes, which "see" the sky in an entirely different way—through detecting radio emissions from outer space. Instead of operating in the visual or near infrared spectrum, radio telescopes operate in the radio frequency area of the **electromagnetic spectrum**. And instead of using large mirrors, radio telescopes use giant **parabolic** (dish-shaped) antennas and can be used in **array**, meaning that a line of telescopes works together to detect radio signals from outer space.

The first radio telescope was developed in 1932, effectively beginning the domain of radio astronomy. After World War II, the development of radar technology used in the war effort was converted to radio astronomy, and great strides were made in the field. Today, one of the largest radio telescopes in the world is the Arecibo radio telescope in Puerto Rico, with a 1,000-foot (305 m) parabolic antenna. Radio telescopes, like optical telescopes, need to be positioned far away from large cities and big populations because of light pollution in the case of optical telescopes, or electromagnetic pollution in the case of radio telescopes. They receive radio emissions from far-away stars and galaxies, as well as other celestial objects, and a radio telescope detected and proved the existence of **cosmic microwave background radiation** (CMB) in 1964, which proved the existence of the big bang.

In 2009, China began construction on the largest radio telescope ever made, the 1,640-foot (500 m) **Aperture** Spherical Telescope (FAST). FAST's completion in September 2016 ushered in a new and exciting time in extreme precision radio astronomy.

OTHER TELESCOPES

In addition to detecting the visual spectrum (light waves) and radio waves, more recent telescopes can detect longer and shorter waves such as gamma rays, X-rays, ultraviolet rays, and infrared radiation. These are all forms of electromagnetic radiation, which are created by all celestial objects that have a temperature above absolute zero. By creating telescopes that can detect these different forms of radiation, astronomers can create a more-detailed view of our universe. For example, it would have been impossible for scientists to find irrefutable evidence of the big bang using only optical telescopes. While early astronomers did use optical telescopes to determine that distant galaxies are moving away from us, thus suggesting there was an initial explosion that propelled them outward, astronomers and astrophysicists debated over what this could mean until they discovered invisible cosmic microwave background radiation. These two pieces of evidence strengthened the big bang theory when they were taken together.

Radio Telescopes and Cosmic Microwave Background Radiation

One of the largest astronomical discoveries of the twentieth century was the detection of cosmic microwave background radiation in 1964. Radio astronomers Arno Penzias and Robert Woodrow Wilson were experimenting with a large 19-foot (6 m) antenna that was built to detect radio signals sent from early satellites. This required a very clear signal, so Penzias and Wilson removed all other forms of radio interference to focus on the radio waves they were looking for.

However, as they were analyzing their data, they realized that, despite all their efforts, they still heard a constant, and relatively loud background noise. What could this be? Penzias soon heard about the work of other astronomers who had theorized that an enormous cosmic event, such as the big bang, should have left over detectable radiation throughout the universe. The specifications that these astronomers theorized fit perfectly with what Penzias and Wilson heard. This was cosmic microwave background radiation, the first direct evidence of the big bang.

Penzias and Wilson received the Nobel Prize in Physics in 1978 for their discovery. Upon receiving his award, Penzias said:

> Throughout most of recorded history, matter was thought to be composed of various combinations of four basic elements: earth, air, fire and water. Modern science has replaced this list with a considerably longer one ... Most of these, the oxygen we breathe, the iron in our blood, the uranium in our reactors, were formed during the fiery lifetimes and explosive deaths of stars in the heavens around us. A few of the elements were formed before the stars even existed, during the birth of the universe itself.

Thus, the discovery of CMB once again shifted the way we not only thought about the big bang, or even the universe itself, but of ourselves and everything that makes up the matter in and around us.

Today, many of these different kinds of telescopes are no longer limited to planet Earth—they are sent into Earth's orbit where they transmit their discoveries back to scientists on the ground. A benefit of optical telescopes in space is that Earth's atmosphere cannot disturb the light that is refracted in the telescope. This means that the images captured by an optical space telescope usually have much higher resolution than ground-based telescopes. A famous example of such a telescope is the Hubble Space Telescope (HST), which was first launched into low Earth orbit in 1990. It remains in orbit today. Using a 7.9-foot (2.9 m) mirror, the HST is able to observe the near ultraviolet, visible, and near infrared spectra. It is well known both inside and outside of the astronomical community and is responsible for major breakthroughs in astronomy since its launch. For example, observations using the HST allowed astrophysicists to determine the expansion rate of the universe.

The telescope was built with funding from NASA, with the aid of the European Space Agency. The Goddard Space Flight Center, a NASA research center in Maryland, controls the telescope. Because of its location, any issues or mechanical adjustments to the telescope must be made by astronauts during servicing missions. Famously, almost immediately after the launch, the HST's main mirror was discovered to have been positioned incorrectly. This was an embarrassing mistake for NASA and created somewhat of a public relations crisis. Finally, a servicing mission was sent out in 1993 to fix the main mirror. Since then, the HST has been in near-continual service. The final servicing mission was approved in 2009. The telescope is expected to continue operating until at least 2030 to 2040. The scheduled launch of the James Webb Space Telescope, a major space observatory that will be a successor to the HST, will be launched in 2018.

One of the most exciting aspects of the Hubble Space Telescope is that anyone can apply to use it! Although it is very competitive to have your application approved, many amateur astronomers have been granted research time on the Hubble, although less and less time has been granted to nonprofessional astronomers in recent years.

SPACE PROBES

Since the launch of *Sputnik*, many more probes have been sent up into outer space. In 1972 and 1973, *Pioneer 10* and *Pioneer 11* were launched to visit Jupiter and Saturn. These missions were immensely successful and provided the first flybys of the gas giants. The missions sent back incredibly clear photographs of Jupiter's big spot and Saturn's rings and even discovered some unknown moons orbiting Saturn.

The next space probes sent after the Pioneer program were *Voyager 1* and *Voyager 2*. They made important discoveries on Jupiter and Saturn, and then went further to conduct the first flybys of Uranus and Neptune. Near Uranus,

An artist's depiction of the *Voyager* spacecraft

the Voyager missions discovered ten new moons; during a flyby of Neptune, their observations were used by scientists to calculate that the planet actually weighs much less than previously thought! Both probes have left our solar system now and have the power to continue further into interstellar space until at least 2025. *Voyager 2* has traveled the farthest distance from Earth than any man-made object in history, and is currently one hundred times farther away from Earth than Earth is from the sun.

The Wilkinson Microwave Anisotrophy Probe (WMAP) mission, launched in 2001, has proved to be one of the most influential space missions ever, although it is not as well known as the Voyager missions. Instead of examining the universe through optical instruments, it measures the temperature of cosmic microwave background radiation in order to map out these temperatures and better understand the distribution of cosmic material following the big bang. One of its most important discoveries is that the universe is older than scientists previously calculated, clocking in at 13.7 billion years. It also confirmed the existence of dark matter and dark energy, and showed that they account for 95 percent of all material in our universe.

One space probe that scans the X-rays present in the universe is the Chandra X-Ray Observatory, launched in 1999. X-ray telescopes need to be space-based, as Earth's atmosphere blocks out most X-rays. X-ray observations allow scientists to study the universe in a much different way, because of the nature of these short-wavelength and high-energy light waves. One interesting discovery made by Chandra was the X-ray remnants of a crushed star after a supernova.

The *Viking 1* probe was the first probe to land successfully on Mars, which it did in July 1976. (Soviet probes had previously landed on Mars but failed upon landing.) *Viking 1* operated on Mars' surface for 6 years and 116 days, becoming the longest-lasting project on the surface of the Red Planet as well. It sent back the world's first color photographs of Mars and allowed scientists to better explore and understand its surface—paving the way for later discoveries that would show evidence of water on Mars.

SPACECRAFT

Nearly sixty years since the beginning of the space race, only three nations have flown manned space missions: the US, Russia, and China.

Since Yuri Gagarin's first trip into space in 1961, there have been many other missions using manned spacecraft. The same year that Gagarin completed his orbit around the Earth, American Alan Shepard completed a sub-orbit of the Earth aboard the *Freedom 7* spacecraft. This fifteen-minute flight was the first US manned spaceflight and paved the way for many more (and longer) missions. This was part of the Mercury program, which lasted from 1958 until 1963, carried a one-man crew, and was followed by the Gemini program. Project Gemini placed ten two-man crews into orbit between 1965 and 1966 and effectively put the United States in the lead, for the first time, in the Space Race against the Soviet Union. But the biggest program was yet to come: Project Apollo. Project Apollo followed on the heels of the Gemini program, which showed scientists and engineers that manned missions could be sustained for the amount of time it would take to orbit the moon. For Project Apollo, their ambitious end goal was to land a man on the moon. And this is what Apollo would become famous for.

Project Apollo began in 1961, largely due to then-president John F. Kennedy's stated goal to land a man on the moon by the end of the 1960s, and ran concurrently with

Gemini until 1966 when the Gemini program concluded. *Apollo* engineers recognized early on that the their current control center at the Cape Canaveral Air Force Station would be inadequate to house and maneuver the larger spacecraft they were using. Construction to build a new mission control center (called the Christopher C. Kraft Jr. Mission Control Center as of 2011) began in the early 1960s and was completed by 1965. Located in Houston, Texas, this mission control center is known by its call designation over the radio: "Houston." Simultaneously, the *Apollo* rocket engineers began to create plans to build large launch vehicles that would provide more lift capacity and send spacecraft higher up into orbit. Known as the Saturn launchers, these rocket boosters were used throughout the Apollo program.

The first manned Apollo mission, however, would end in tragedy. *Apollo 1* was planned for launch on February 21, 1967, with the astronauts Virgil "Gus" Grissom, Edward White, and Roger Chaffee. On a rehearsal test on January 27 at Cape Kennedy Air Force Station, the aircraft was detached from all outside cables and relied only on internal power to see how it would operate during the planned mission. This test was not considered dangerous. The three astronauts entered into the spacecraft and the hatch was closed. After several hours of conducting normal test procedures, one of the astronauts shouted that a fire had erupted inside. Unfortunately, fueled by combustible pure oxygen in the cabin, the fire grew very hot very quickly, and rescue workers were not able to reach the three astronauts, who did not survive. A later investigation revealed that faulty wiring in the cabin was most likely to blame.

Following this horrific accident, there was public outcry in the United States about continuing the space program at the risk of astronauts' lives. President Lyndon B. Johnson, who succeeded President John F. Kennedy following his assassination in 1963, was a staunch defender of the Apollo mission and was able to convince politicians and American citizens to continue to support the program. Following *Apollo 1*, NASA focused on several unmanned operations to continue to test its spacecraft for a period of twenty-one months. The next manned Apollo mission was *Apollo 7*, which launched on October 11, 1968. *Apollo 7*, carrying crew members Walter Schirra, Donn Eisele, and Walter Cunningham, was the first manned Apollo mission that sent astronauts into space. Their mission was a "test" flight, to test the *Apollo* Command Module while orbiting the Earth for eleven days. This mission was a success. *Apollo 7* was seen as giving the confidence to NASA to launch *Apollo 8*, which would send three astronauts to leave Earth's orbit for the first time and complete an orbit around the moon.

On December 21, 1968, *Apollo 8* was launched from the Kennedy Space Center with Frank Borman, James Lovell, and William Anders aboard. This was the first manned flight that used the powerful *Saturn V* rocket, which used three stages to launch the spacecraft into orbit. Each stage contained its own engines and propellants, which then would drop off before the firing of the next stage of the rocket, thereby allowing the rocket more lift while carrying less weight. Once they reached orbit, the astronauts performed routine tasks to test the spacecraft and then jettisoned the remaining rocket. They would need this as they would take the command module back down to Earth. Before rotating away from Earth, the astronauts turned to look back at their planet; this was the first time any human had seen the whole Earth.

It took three days for *Apollo 8* to reach the moon. The crew remained housed in the cabin of the command module, which is what they would use to return to Earth. The service module, which was part of the command module, provided the astronauts with propulsion and electrical power, as well as storage, during their mission. *Apollo 8* was also supposed to have the lunar module with them as a test, which was the machine built to bring two crew members to the surface of the moon and back to the command module. However, the lunar module was not ready in time for the launch of *Apollo 8* and so the mission was scheduled without it.

After the *Apollo 8* crew began their maneuvers to enter into the moon's orbit, they had to ignite the service module's engine for exactly four minutes and thirteen seconds. If they ignited the engine for too long, they could have exited the moon's orbit and been flung off into far space. Too short a time, and they would crash into the moon. During their time orbiting the far side of the moon, they were not in radio contact with Earth. The crew later described this time as the longest—and most stressful—time of their lives. Finally, they emerged from the dark side of the moon, taking pictures of Earth as it rose up past the surface of the moon. During their ninth orbit, the crew began the world's first television transmission from space, during which they described the experience of orbiting the moon, read prayers, and send a Christmas message of peace to all those on Earth.

Of course, another record would soon be tested, the entire reason for the Apollo program: landing the first men on the moon. *Apollo 11* launched on July 16, 1969, with Neil Armstrong, Buzz Aldrin, and Michael Collins on board. Like *Apollo 8*, *Apollo 11* was launched by a *Saturn V* rocket from the Kennedy Space Center and consisted of different parts: a command module, a service module, and, unlike *Apollo 8*, a lunar module. After the rockets were used up and jettisoned, crew members in the command module would use the service module for propulsion and support, including oxygen and electrical power. The lunar module, which the crew members had named *Eagle*, would be separated from the rest of the spacecraft and piloted by Buzz Aldrin down to the surface of the moon.

Following a three-day journey to the moon, Aldrin and Armstrong entered into *Eagle* and separated from the command module, where Michael Collins remained. Aldrin steered toward the moon in a controlled "burn." When the lunar module finally touched down on the moon, Armstrong radioed to Houston, stating, "The *Eagle* has landed." Over the next several hours, Armstrong and Aldrin prepared for the first moonwalk in history. A mounted camera aboard the lunar module broadcast as Armstrong slowly climbed down the ladder to the surface of the moon, stating the famous words "That's one small step for [a] man, one giant leap for mankind."

The Apollo mission had succeeded in its goal of putting an American man on the moon, and the Space Race was over. Americans watched in awe as the astronauts moved around the surface of the moon, and then-president Richard Nixon called the astronauts in what he would deem "the most historic phone call ever made from the White House." Aldrin and Armstrong left tributes on the surface of the moon, including a statue to the fallen astronauts who had come before them, and the flag of the United States. They also collected moon dust and rocks to be brought back to Earth for testing and left behind machines to conduct future scientific research. Then the *Eagle* ascended to rendezvous with the command module and begin the return flight to Earth.

The night before splashdown, where the command module would renter Earth's surface and plunge into

Buzz Aldrin explores the lunar surface during the Apollo 11 mission.

the Pacific Ocean, Collins commented on the amazing machinery that had put him and his fellow crew members into outer space—and on the moon. He said:

> *The Saturn V rocket which put us in orbit is an incredibly complicated piece of machinery, every piece of which worked flawlessly ... We have always had confidence that this equipment will work properly. All this is possible only through the blood, sweat, and tears of a number of people ... All you see is the three of us, but beneath the surface are thousands and thousands of others, and to all of those, I would like to say, "Thank you very much."*

Scientists transport part of the
James Webb Telescope at NASA.

3

Scientists, Mathematicians, and Engineers

S ince the political motivations behind the Space
Race first spurred on the development of new space
technology, NASA has become one of the largest actors
in recent space exploration. Scientists, mathematicians,
and engineers employed at NASA, a federal agency, have
developed many of the tools that we now rely on to explore
our universe. This is because, traditionally, the federal
government has been able to use its budget to develop
important technologies that can cost millions of dollars. In
the past, large research universities, such as Caltech, have
also been largely instrumental in developing new space
technologies. This is because, like with a federal agency
such as NASA, universities receive a large amount of their
funding from the federal government. In addition to this,
universities can use their endowments, as well as money

raised from tuition and fundraising, to pay their scientists and to fund the development of large scientific projects. Of course, making very complex astronomical machinery is no longer a matter of using small pieces of metal and glass to build a telescope. Today's machines are incredibly complex and are built from materials that cost a lot of money to produce. In addition to this, scientists, mathematicians, and engineers must be paid to develop an idea or to begin designing or constructing an idea. All of this means that developing new space technology costs an astounding amount of money.

In recent years, a weakened US economy has led to federal budget cuts, which have, in turn, led to decreased funds allocated for research and development at NASA. Science advocates have mentioned that public perception of how much federal money goes to fund NASA's projects is grossly overestimated; while American perception, according to polls, is that 20 percent of the federal budget goes to NASA, in actuality, less than 1 percent does. For the 2016 **fiscal** year, less than 5 percent of the budget is allocated to NASA. There are estimates that state that Americans spend less than nine dollars a year in tax allocated to NASA. Despite this, funding has steadily decreased in past years, making it difficult to fund the ambitious technologies that first landed a man on the moon in 1969.

Partly due to the budgetary crisis, in recent years private organizations have begun to focus on space exploration and spacecraft manufacturing. SpaceX is a notable example of this. Created by Elon Musk, a famous entrepreneur and the founder of Tesla Motors, SpaceX is a privately funded corporation that has been supported by its investors. In recent years, SpaceX has made and met ambitious plans in developing reusable rockets; instead of jettisoning rockets once in orbit, SpaceX rockets are developed to return back to Earth and to be reused in subsequent missions. While SpaceX's budget is still much less than NASA's total funding, this design has allowed SpaceX to spend much less money on rebuilding new rockets. So far, the model has shown promising results although, as of yet, no manned missions have been launched.

While it may be somewhat depressing to think of scientific research in terms of funding, budget constraints are a very real pressure on astronomical research and development today. Unfortunately, money is needed to incubate ideas, experiment, design, and manufacture new technologies.

This chapter will explore important scientists, mathematicians, and engineers who are working for federal agencies such as NASA, in research universities, or through private organizations to develop the tools that will enrich our understanding of our universe.

NASA

Few names of the scientists who worked tirelessly at NASA, pioneering humankind's first voyage to the moon and other important missions, are well known. According to Edward C. Stone, Jet Propulsion Laboratory Director and Voyager project scientist, NASA scientists come from diverse backgrounds and bring in diverse skill sets, but they must share "qualities like patience, dedication, optimism, faith in colleagues, a willingness to take informed risks, and the capacity to be a team player." The ability to be a team player is of the utmost importance for incredibly complex projects like sending a spacecraft into outer space. This is because there are many different factors and areas of expertise that must be taken into account. Mechanical engineers, for example, are necessary during the construction of spacecraft, as well as physicists, mathematicians, and astrophysicists. The computers on board a spacecraft must be made by a computer engineer or a flight software designer. Climate scientists need to examine weather patterns to make sure a launch day will go according to plan, while geologists need to study the surface of the moon or lend their expertise to the way a lunar excursion vehicle will touch down on Martian soil.

James Van Allen was a space scientist and physicist who became the principal investigator for over twenty-four NASA missions over the course of his career. Born in Iowa

James Van Allen *(right)* speaks during a Pioneer news conference in 1973.

in 1914, Van Allen earned his doctorate degree in physics
from the University of Iowa in 1939. In 1951, he became a
professor there and eventually became head of the Physics
and Astronomy department. During his tenure, he conducted
research that initiated the burgeoning field of magnetospheric
research in space, which examines the magnetic fields around
the Earth that protect us from dangerous charged particles
emitted by the sun. His research on using rockets and so-
called "rockoons," or rockets carried into space by balloons,
explored the behavior of cosmic rays in the atmosphere.
These experiments drew the attention of NASA in 1957.
That same year, Van Allen played an important role in the

International Geophysical Year, which ended in 1958 with the launch of the *Explorer 1*. Van Allen's experiments were conducted aboard the spacecraft with a Geiger-Muller tube to detect radiation around Earth. This was the beginning of magnetospheric research and would prove to be important to future space missions, especially in regard to studying the potentially dangerous radiation astronauts might be exposed to and the turbulence that can be experienced by spacecraft in flight. Van Allen won many awards throughout his career for his contributions to astronomical research and to space science in particular. He won the Daniel and Florence Guggenheim International Astronautical Award in 1962 and the Smithsonian National Air and Space Museum Trophy for lifetime achievement in 2006. In 1994, Van Allen received the Gerard P. Kuiper Prize from the American Astronomical Society. That same year, he was awarded a lifetime achievement award by NASA. In 1989, he received the Crafoord Prize by the Royal Swedish Academy of Sciences. This award is the equivalent to the Nobel Prize for space science.

Van Allen's research enabled many flights, including *Pioneer 10* and *Pioneer 11*. As Lou Friedman, founder and executive director of Planetary Society, remarked, "[Jim Van Allen] was a pioneer who helped give birth to the space age and later enabled many great spacefaring adventures and helped open up the outer solar system for exploration.

Anyone who knew him was privileged." James Van Allen passed away at the age of ninety-one in 2006.

Many others contributed to these important early space missions, including Bob Gilruth, an aeronautical engineer who acted as the director of the Manned Spacecraft Center at NASA from the Mercury through Apollo missions. His skill at managing diverse groups of people in his team is often stated as one of the successes of the early space program. Margaret Hamilton, a mathematician at MIT, was also instrumental in the early space program. Before computer science was a common course of study, Hamilton was tasked with creating the onboard flight software that would bring the first astronauts to the moon. Through Hamilton's pioneering research, she would coin the new term "software engineering." Hamilton developed a new computer language, Universal Systems Language, and a formal systems theory, both of which allowed her and her team to create software that was reliable enough to land a crew safely on the moon. Hamilton was extremely rigorous in developing the software: she developed priority displays, which would interrupt the astronauts in flight if the computer detected any emergency during the mission, allowing them to reset the computer to avert disaster. Hamilton ran her software through every possible worst-case scenario and had multiple lines of testing from development to production.

Later, Hamilton reflected on her work during the Apollo program:

> *There was no second chance. We all knew that. We took our work very seriously, but we were young, many of us in our 20s. Coming up with new ideas was an adventure. Dedication and commitment were a given. Mutual respect was across the board. Because software was a mystery, a black box, upper management gave us total freedom and trust. We had to find a way and we did. Looking back, we were the luckiest people in the world; there was no choice but to be pioneers; no time to be beginners.*

Indeed, Hamilton's software worked flawlessly during the *Apollo 11* moon landing. The software alerted the astronauts to a problem right before landing on the moon, which overrode the error and safely landed the *Eagle* on the lunar surface.

In 1959, NASA ordered a young team of scientists to build the first spacecraft ever made. John R. Casani headed a team of young engineers, including Marc Comuntzis, Walter Downhower, and James Burke, with the job of building a "planetary machine." Comuntizis and Downhower, with help from John H. Gerpheide and Bill Layman, would design the overall structure of the probes. Steve Szirmay and Ted Kopf were electronic engineers who would work on the avionics technology in the spacecraft to make sure it could maintain balance and orientation in space. Another team of electronic engineers developed the so-called "armor" to the spacecraft, so that it could be protected from the harsh environment of outer space. Yet another team of electronic engineers would be tasked particularly with providing the infrastructure through which mission control on Earth could communicate with the spacecraft. Propulsion engineers Duane Dipprey and Dave Evans developed new rocket technology to create long duration systems that were incredibly reliable. Yet another team focused on power generation, allowing a shift from solar power to batteries and back again. Then there were the teams of scientists who had to calculate the mechanics of outer space in order to create the conditions for a space rendezvous. Mathematician Clarence R. Gates and engineers Charles Kolhause, Norman R. Haynes, Vic Clarke, John Beckman, and William Melbourne calculated conditions and navigated paths through space. A Deep Space Instrumentation Facility system designer, Walter Victor, along with his team of engineers established a network of receivers across locations on Earth so that the spacecraft would continually be in contact with Earth unless it passed behind a celestial body like the moon.

One of their earliest breakthroughs was deciding that, rather than having a spacecraft that would spin for stability, they would move the spacecraft along three different axes. Movements would be much more precise than earlier probes were designed. The team first developed *Ranger*, a probe that was sent to the moon. The earliest *Ranger*s that the team designed were unsuccessful, mostly because of rocket failures. However, each of these failures taught the team something new, and they would tweak their next designs to fix previous errors. By the end of their project in 1965, the team had garnered a lot of experience and collected many images from their spacecraft, even if their ultimate missions had failed. Then, Casani and his team worked on developing *Mariner*, the first probe destined for Venus and Mars.

THE LANGLEY RESEARCH CENTER

The Langley Research Center was established long before NASA and the space program in 1917. In fact, according to NASA, "Langley gave birth to key components of the US space program." Beginning in 1952, research scientists at Langley began to think seriously about sending humans into space. A study into this possibility is what led to the development of Project Mercury. While many people have heard of Langley, few can name the scientists and engineers there who developed the important technology used to eventually land a man on the moon. One of the engineers at Langley, John Houbolt, has been called an "unsung hero of the Apollo program" and is credited with developing the lunar module and advancing the idea of lunar-orbit rendezvous, in which the lunar lander would independently

John Houbolt explains diagrams showing his proposed space rendezvous for lunar missions in 1962.

land on the surface of the moon after disconnecting from the main command module. This made it possible to safely land the first astronauts on the surface of the moon, and Houbolt is often directly credited with the success of the Apollo 11 mission. However, when Houbolt first spoke out about the idea, it was considered irrational and dangerous.

Houbolt was born in Iowa in 1919 and graduated from the University of Illinois at Urbana-Champaign with a bachelor's and master's degree in civil engineering. He later received a PhD. He began working at Langley in 1942 as an engineer. Since 1959, Houbolt had been studying the technical details of rendezvous in space and the so-called lunar-orbit rendezvous. He was convinced that, using this technique, NASA could land astronauts on the moon and return them back safely using existing technology. Houbolt was one of the first and only engineers at Langley who thought this would be feasible; other scientists thought that they would need to develop a giant rocket or to launch multiple rocket ships that would then assemble a lunar ship in space. All of this, however, would take too much time to develop because the technology did not yet exist.

Convinced that he had the answer to landing American astronauts on the moon, Houbolt sent a letter to one of the head scientists at Langley. He wrote:

> Do we want to go to the moon or not? Why is Nova [the giant rocket launcher], with its ponderous size simply just accepted, and why is a much less grandiose scheme involving rendezvous ostracized or put on the defensive? I fully realize that contacting you in this manner is somewhat unorthodox, but the issues at stake are crucial enough to us all that an unusual course is warranted.

It was not just Houbolt's insight that allowed him to champion this idea, but his bravery when no one else believed in him.

Houbolt's main design change was to use the current technology of the *Saturn V* rocket launcher to launch "an assembly" of three different spacecraft into Earth's orbit. A command module would hold the main controls and cabin; the service module would hold the main engine, fuel cells, and the altitude control system; and a lunar module would be used for lunar excursions. The lunar module would fit two crewmembers who would use it to descend to the surface of the moon. Then, following the lunar excursion, the lunar module would return to the command module and dock. Once the two crewmembers rejoined the command module, the lunar module would either be jettisoned off into space or crashed back onto the surface of the moon.

Houbolt continued to champion his idea until he convinced the Langley higher-ups that it was the only method that could land astronauts on the surface of the moon by the end of the 1960s. Then came many years of testing. Most essential was perfecting the docking of the lunar module with the command module. Scientists were frightened that this would be the most difficult step in the mission. Their secret fear was that the astronauts would successfully land on the moon but then would be stuck in the lunar module, unable to be saved; then the one crewmember in the command module, unable to save his two other crewmembers, would be forced to abandon them and return to Earth alone. To prevent this catastrophic scenario, Langley engineers built several different simulators. The Rendezvous Docking Simulator, which Houbolt oversaw, allowed the engineers, scientists, and astronauts to perfect these techniques before embarking on the Apollo 11 mission. This was the key to the successful moon landing.

Another challenge was building the lunar module itself. Langley engineers knew that the module would need to be controlled by many small rockets. Because of the moon's lack of gravity, they would need to adjust the thrust of the engines so that it was only one-sixth as powerful as an equivalent machine would need to be on Earth. Finally, the pilot astronaut of the lunar module would need to know how to control such a machine—difficult because of the use of many small rockets—and in an atmosphere totally different than Earth's. To address these issues, Langley constructed the Lunar Landing Research Facility in 1965. They built lunar module simulators and produced, using an overhead suspension system, extremely low-gravity conditions with the simulator to reproduce conditions on the moon. Over the decade, twenty-four different astronauts, including Neil Armstrong and Buzz Aldrin, practiced in these facilities. Other simulators and entire facilities were also developed during this time, including facilities dedicated to exploring the possibility of an impact on the moon, the effect of blowing lunar dust on pilot response, vertical braking maneuvers, and other specialized techniques.

Of course, the successful *Apollo 11* moon landing was the result of many different scientists, mathematicians, and engineers working together. Each one performed an integral task, although many are not known by name today. Among some of the most well-known scientists to contribute to the Apollo space program was Katherine Johnson, a physicist and mathematician who performed important calculations to ensure the accuracy of launches and landings. Before Apollo, Johnson successfully calculated the space flight trajectory for the first American in space, Alan Shepard, in 1959. She later calculated important launch windows for the Mercury mission in 1961. She also calculated the trajectory for the *Apollo* moon landing. Without Johnson's expertise, the mission would have ended in failure. Calculating the accurate trajectory is one of the most fundamental aspects of space flight. For *Apollo 13*, when the mission to the moon was aborted due to mechanical failures, Johnson's calculations allowed the astronauts to return safely to Earth. Johnson spent decades working at NASA after earning her PhD in math. Throughout her career, she authored more than twenty-eight scientific papers. She was awarded the Presidential Medal of Freedom in 2015 for her pioneering work as an African American woman in science.

Katherine Johnson ensured successful space missions with her accurate calculations.

SPACEX

Space Exploration Technologies Corporation, better known as SpaceX, has led a new era of spaceflight since its founding in 2002. The brainchild of Tesla and PayPal entrepreneur Elon Musk, SpaceX was developed to reduce the cost of space transportation and to eventually enable Mars colonization. While this idea may sound farfetched, SpaceX has been hitting its goals and has developed some of the most powerful rockets in use today. Tom Mueller, the head of rocket design at SpaceX, is often credited with developing the technology to reach many firsts in the industry, including being the first company to succeed at landing its rocket back on Earth vertically after an **orbital** flight.

Tom Mueller began working at SpaceX as a rocket scientist soon after its inception. Born in Idaho, Mueller wanted to be a logger, like his father, when he grew up. But he also had a deep interest as a child in model rockets. He continued to experiment with building and launching different rockets throughout his childhood.

After receiving his bachelor's degree in mechanical engineering, Mueller moved to California and began working first on satellite designs before beginning to develop liquid-powered rocket engines. He was the lead engineer during the development of the TR-106 rocket engine, using hydrogen, which was one of the most powerful engines ever developed at that time. Frustrated with the constraints of his corporation, Mueller began to experiment with liquid-fueled rocket engines in his garage after work, eventually designing and building the largest amateur liquid-powered rocket engine in existence. The attention that Mueller received from this project drew the interest of Elon Musk, who was developing his idea for the SpaceX company. He approached Mueller and offered him a job as a founding employee in the new company. Mueller accepted the offer in 2002 and joined SpaceX.

Mueller is now Vice President of Propulsion Development at SpaceX. He has developed propulsion systems for most of the rockets that SpaceX has become known for, including the *Dragon* spacecraft and the Merlin rocket engine family. The *Dragon* was the first commercially built and operated spacecraft to be recovered following a successful mission after its first flight in 2010. In 2012, it became the first commercial spacecraft to dock at the International Space Station.

VIRGIN GALACTIC

Many other companies have also set their sights on developing commercial spaceflights. Virgin Galactic is a large spaceflight company developed in 2004 by Virgin Group and Virgin Atlantic airline founder Richard Branson. Branson hoped to build aircrafts particularly for space tourists, or regular civilians who pay to go to space for recreational purposes. Along with aerospace engineer and founder of aerospace company Scaled Composites, Burt Rutan, Branson founded The Spaceship Company in 2005 (it has since become a sole subsidiary of Virgin Galactic). Rutan had previously developed *SpaceShipOne*, an air-launched aircraft that completed the first manned private spaceflight on June 21, 2004, when it flew 62.5 miles (100.6 km) above Earth to the frontier of space. Two more flights followed in 2004, winning *SpaceShipOne* the coveted $10 million Ansari X Prize.

SpaceShipOne was notable not just for completing this trip, but for its design. This reusable spacecraft measured 28 feet (8.5 m) and was about 5 feet (1.5 m) in diameter, large enough to carry a pilot and two crewmembers. It used a special "feathering" reentry system, in which the rear half of its large, wide wings would fold back and up to increase drag and stability. This allowed the aircraft to land safely back on Earth and, thus, to be reused for subsequent flights.

Also unique was the way in which *SpaceShipOne* was launched—in mid-air. Attached to the bottom of its "mothership," called the *White Knight*, *SpaceShipOne* was designed to glide first upon separation before firing hybrid rocket motors for a period of eighty seconds. These motors use both solid and liquid propellants and powered the rocket ship past Earth's atmosphere. From there, *SpaceShipOne* spent three minutes in space before gliding safely back down to Earth in approximately twenty minutes. The pilot of *SpaceShipOne*, Mike Melville, became the first commercial space pilot ever following his successful spaceflight.

After *SpaceShipOne*, Branson and Butan teamed up to build a new version of the successful spacecraft: *SpaceShipTwo*. *SpaceShipTwo* is larger and is designed to carry two pilots and six passengers on short **suborbital** spaceflights. The time in space (and, thus, in weightlessness) would only amount to several minutes. Similar to *SpaceShipOne*, it is launched in midair from its mothership, the *White Knight Two*, and glides

The Jet Propulsion Laboratory

NASA's Jet Propulsion Laboratory (JPL) is a robotic spacecraft research and development center in collaboration with Caltech in Pasadena, California. The laboratory is currently working on ten different missions, including the *Curiosity* rover to Mars, the Juno mission to Jupiter, and the development of new telescopes, including the NuSTAR X-ray telescope and the Spitzer Space Telescope. In particular, the JPL's rovers to Mars are being used to collect data for NASA's future manned missions to the Red Planet.

Although the JPL is a working laboratory and not a museum, you can schedule a free, guided tour by reserving in advance. Tours last for several hours and include a multimedia presentation on JPL entitled "Journey to the Planets and Beyond." While at JPL, visitors can also visit the von Karman Visitor Center, the Space Flight Operations Facility, and the Spacecraft Assembly Facility. It's a wonderful opportunity to see how scientists and engineers develop, design, and produce the next generation of spacecraft!

down to Earth on a conventional landing. Virgin Galactic operates two of these spacecraft (with plans to build three more) and has taken bookings, which cost $250,000 per ticket, for several years. Passengers who have already paid deposits for future missions include celebrities like Brad Pitt and Angelina Jolie, as well as scientist Stephen Hawking.

However, Virgin Galactic suffered a major setback in 2014 when a test flight of the first *SpaceShipTwo* model, called the *VSS Enterprise*, broke up in flight approximately one minute after launch and crashed into the Mojave desert, killing its copilot. A new model was unveiled in February 2016 and is undergoing testing before its first flight at the time of this writing.

Virgin Galactic has also built an orbit launch vehicle, called *LauncherOne*, which can launch 440 pounds (200 kilograms) of payloads into Earth orbit. Commercial customers such as satellite companies can pay to launch their equipment into orbit. As of 2016, they are on schedule to begin test flights of *LauncherOne* and have signed contracts with multiple satellite companies for future launches. Virgin Galactic has also signed an agreement with NASA for potential collaboration in research flights.

It appears as if collaboration between not only multiple teams of scientists, engineers, and mathematicians will enable our future explorations in space, but also collaborations between space agencies, universities, and private companies, as well.

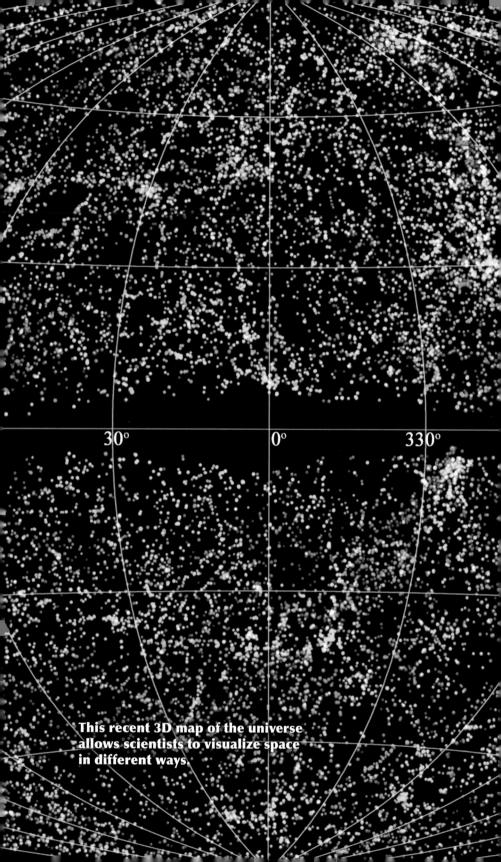

30°   0°   330°

This recent 3D map of the universe
allows scientists to visualize space
in different ways.

Visualizing Space with Current Technology

T hese new technologies have not just helped us understand our universe better and our place in it—or even just challenged us to explore the universe in more innovative and exciting ways. These technologies have allowed us to "see" the universe better. At the beginning of the twentieth century, our understanding of the universe was that it was entirely composed of our own galaxy, the Milky Way, and that we were at the center of all matter that existed in the universe. This was similar to the seventeenth-century belief that the Earth stood at the center of the universe in the geocentric model that preceded Copernicus's revolution.

In the early part of the twentieth century, even with the new technology of large telescopes like the Hale Telescope, most astronomers still believed our whole universe was only composed fully of the Milky Way galaxy and that it was much smaller than we now know it to be. The size and scope of our universe was unimaginable to most back then. Then Edwin Hubble turned the Hale Telescope to the sky. His observations proved to the world that stars we had previously thought to be part of our own galaxy were actually much farther away and in different galaxies. Following his discovery, our notion of the size and scope of our universe changed drastically.

With these astronomical discoveries came bigger philosophical questions. What does it mean if we are no longer the center of our solar system or the center of our universe? If we are one of a near infinite number of galaxies (and, thus, planets), are we as special as we thought we were?

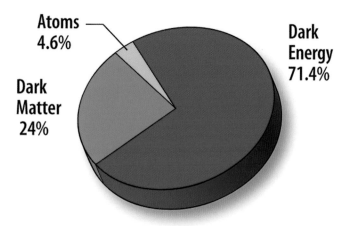

This pie chart shows how little of our universe is made up of atoms and "visible" matter.

These questions came to light again with a more recent discovery using the more sophisticated telescopes of the late twentieth and early twenty-first century. In 1998, two research teams simultaneously and independently used their observations to determine that the universe has not just been expanding since the big bang—but it has been accelerating, hurtling outward at faster speeds. Why is this important? Because of something called dark energy, which is the invisible force some astronomers state is pushing this acceleration. Current models show that nearly 73 percent of the mass and energy present in the universe comes from dark energy. Of the remaining 30 percent of the mass and energy in our universe, nearly 23 percent comes from dark matter, a mysterious kind of matter that is completely invisible and undetectable on the electromagnetic spectrum. That means that only 4 percent of all matter in our universe is "visible" to us, or made up of ordinary, or baryonic, matter, which means it is made up of atoms. Everything we see around us is made up of baryonic matter, including ourselves. And, yet, the entirety of everything that we see only makes up about 4 percent of all matter and energy in the universe. This is another sea change for astronomy, particularly observational astronomy. As science writer Richard Panek wrote in 2010:

> *For thousands of years our species has studied the night sky and wondered if anything else is out there. Last year we celebrated the 400th anniversary of Galileo's answer: Yes. Galileo trained a new instrument, the telescope, on the heavens and saw*

objects that no other person had ever seen: hundreds
of stars, mountains on the Moon, satellites of Jupiter.
Since then we have found more than 400 planets
around other stars, 100 billion stars in our galaxy,
hundreds of billions of galaxies beyond our own, even
the faint radiation that is the echo of the Big Bang.

Now scientists think that even this extravagant
census of the universe might be as out-of-date as
the five-planet cosmos that Galileo inherited from
the ancients. Astronomers have compiled evidence
that what we've always thought of as the actual
universe—me, you, this magazine, planets, stars,
galaxies, all the matter in space—represents a mere
4 percent of what's actually out there. The rest they
call, for want of a better word, dark: 23 percent is
something they call dark matter, and 73 percent is
something even more mysterious, which they call
dark energy.

What will the future look like if our instruments need to
detect energy and matter that we cannot detect on our own?
How can we render the "invisible" majority of mass and energy
in our universe "visible"? These are questions astrophysicists
and engineers are working on today as they develop new
technology to help us understand these new and mysterious
forces we are only just beginning to understand in our universe.

THE CYCLE OF UNDERSTANDING

The exciting part of current astronomical technology is just
this: As powerful machines enable us to "see" our universe

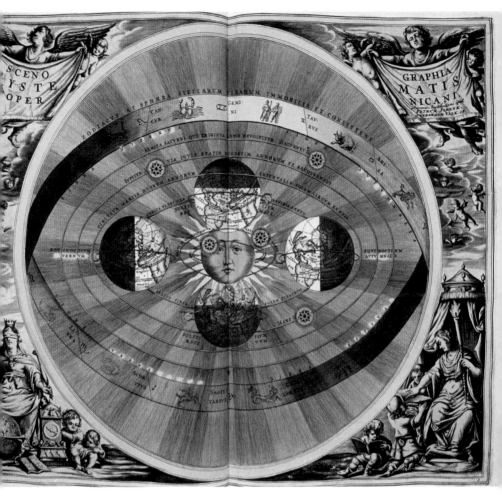

The Copernican model of our solar system correctly theorized that Earth revolved around the sun.

and our place in it differently, teams of scientists are then able to analyze this data and gauge its significance. Then, scientists, engineers, and mathematicians use this new information (and, particularly, their interpretation of this information) in order to develop and build new technologies to further explore these theories, ideas, and scientific developments. This is a cycle that requires both powerful machines and powerful human minds, working in tandem for long periods of time on one challenge. Oftentimes, this is referred to as theoretical versus experimental research. For example, Nicolaus Copernicus formulated a model of the known universe (what we now call the solar system) with the sun at its center, instead of Earth, in 1543. This was a theoretical experiment in which Copernicus used mathematical calculations to show why his model of the solar system was correct. However, this was not proved until Galileo used his telescope to observe the motions of the stars and proved that the heliocentric model Copernicus had proposed was indeed correct. Galileo thus became one of the first observational astronomers.

Albert Einstein, like Copernicus, also used mathematics and theoretical research to understand and "see" the universe. His early theories were based on mathematical predictions. Einstein, unlike Galileo, was not an observational astronomer, and he relied on his calculations to understand the motions of the stars. However, his predictions and theories were proved correct with later astronomical observations. Einstein's theories are still being proven today, and some of the most exciting arenas of future astronomical research are being conducted based on calculations Einstein made nearly one hundred years ago. Thus, the cycle of

understanding in scientific research continually evolves:
humans develop theories, these theories are tested by
machines that observe our universe and provide scientists
with data, and then new scientists analyze this data and
create new hypotheses and theories. This cycle continues
ad infinitum.

OUR NEW VISION OF THE UNIVERSE

Many new projects are attempting to visualize this new
understanding of our universe, which is not composed mainly
of common matter, as previously thought, but is largely
made up of mysterious substances called dark matter and
dark energy. Perhaps someday this new knowledge will have
an impact on manned spaceflight, or be further explored
by long-distance manned missions, but, as of right now,
scientists are using probes and nonoptical telescopes, such as
radio telescopes, to map our universe.

Currently, research into dark matter and dark energy is
largely in the theoretical phase of research. Scientists and
mathematicians have theoretically proved that these forms of
matter exist with mathematical calculations and modeling.
However, because this matter cannot be observed in typical
ways, it has not been backed up by observational research—
at least as of yet. This is the stage of new and complex
machines, whose main task is to provide data to scientists

The Victor M. Blanco Telescope at the Cerro Tololo Inter-American Observatory

to independently prove the existence of these new forms of matter.

One main project that is focused specifically on dark energy is the Dark Energy Survey (DES). Led by scientist Josh Frieman and conducted at the Cerro Tololo Inter-American Observatory in Chile, this project aims to "map hundreds of millions of galaxies, detect thousands of supernovae, and find patterns of cosmic structure that will reveal the nature of the mysterious dark energy that is accelerating the expansion of our Universe."

The DES website succinctly explains the theoretical basis for dark energy, based on Einstein's predictions regarding the gravity of large, cosmic bodies:

> *According to Einstein's theory of General Relativity, gravity should lead to a slowing of the cosmic expansion. Yet, in 1998, two teams of astronomers studying distant supernovae made the remarkable discovery that the expansion of the universe is speeding up. To explain cosmic acceleration, cosmologists are faced with two possibilities: either 70% of the universe exists in exotic form, now called dark energy, that exhibits a gravitational force opposite to the attractive gravity of ordinary matter, or General Relativity must be replaced by a new theory of gravity on cosmic scales.*

Using the Dark Energy Camera, a sensitive 570-megapixel digital camera mounted on the Blanco telescope at Cerro Tololo, the DES team has been taking pictures of huge swaths of the sky. (Imagine the power of the Dark Energy Camera compared to the average 16-pixel camera!) From 2013 until the 2018 program end date, the camera will record information from three hundred million galaxies. Once completed, teams of scientists will begin analyzing the data for further observational proof of

The International Space Station and Dark Matter

While the hunt for dark matter in space is normally done separately from manned space missions, dark matter and manned spaceflight have merged aboard the International Space Station. Since 2011, the Alpha Magnetic Spectrometer (AMS-02) has been mounted to the ISS and has conducted experiments to measure the amount of dark matter in the universe. AMS-02 was launched aboard the space shuttle *Endeavor* in 2011 as part of its final flight. Crewmembers, led by commander Mark Kelly, successfully installed AMS-02 on day four of the mission. This marked the second to last mission of NASA's Space Shuttle program.

In 2013, Nobel Prize winner Samuel Ting of the Massachusetts Institute of Technology (MIT) announced that AMS-02 had detected more than 400,000 positrons, the antimatter equivalent to electrons, which "could be a sign of dark matter." Scientists suspect that positrons can be created by collisions between dark matter, although more research needs to be done to prove this theory.

Ting stated, "So far the evidence supports the hypothesis of dark matter. [But we] need more data at higher energies to decide … the correct explanation. It is only a matter of time, perhaps months or a few years."

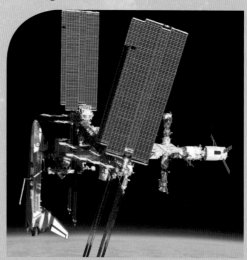

The space shuttle Endeavor docked to the International Space Station in 2011.

dark energy. In fact, a team has already begun preliminary research on 1 percent of the data collected so far. Led by Vinu Vikram, this team was looking for the so-called "smearing effect" of dark matter on common matter. The gravity exerted by dark matter can distort the light emitted from galaxies, although this effect is very small. However, if you have a large amount of data, the effect becomes easier to observe. Vikram's team created a two-dimensional dark matter map based on their results. This map is only a small part of the data that has and will be collected through the DES project, but it is an exciting visualization of the data to come.

After these complex technologies provide data on dark matter and dark energy, scientists will use this data not only to map the universe, as Vikram and his team are beginning to do, but they will also form new hypotheses about the composition of these mysterious forms of matter and energy. Scientists don't know yet what exactly dark energy and dark matter are, what they are composed of, and how exactly they interact with common matter around them. Observational data for dark matter and dark energy will need to be evaluated to shed light on these outstanding questions. In the meantime, probes, cameras, and telescopes are helping observational scientists uncover the mysteries of our universe, while developmental scientists and engineers and working on missions to change humankind's position in it.

An artist's depiction of *Dragon* landing on the Martian surface

5

Space Technology Today and Tomorrow

The future of spaceflight is exciting—one that will, most likely, open up space exploration to regular people instead of highly-trained specialists and astronauts. Our new focus is no longer bringing humans to the moon but even farther: NASA and private companies, including SpaceX and Virgin Galactic, are planning to fly humans to Mars. Even more exciting—and even frightening—is the possibility of more than just short trips into space. NASA and others are now planning to send long-term settlers to Mars by the 2030s. In preparation for this longer-term goal, NASA and others are planning to send humans back to the moon by 2020. In these plans, the moon could be used as a forward base on the way to Mars.

Exciting research that has shown that water is flowing on Mars has contributed to the fervor to colonize the red planet, as well as the belief that the planet can support life. Elon Musk and Richard Branson have been vocal about their plans to land humans on Mars, and Apollo astronaut Buzz Aldrin has been, too. One company that is at the forefront of a potential Mars mission is Mars One, a Dutch company that has famously selected people to train for a one-way mission to Mars. Mission participants would be tasked with creating a permanent base there, and they would never return to Earth. Mars One has received funding from private investors and used crowdfunding to raise additional funds, although full investment information has not been released by the company. Mars One has also been criticized by scientists and officials for moving ahead too quickly without fully examining safety and ethical concerns.

As of 2016, NASA has announced its plans for an "Earth independent" Mars colony by the 2030s. A full report released by NASA compares the plans to establish a Mars colony to early explorers setting out to "discover" land and the moon landing. It states, "Like the Apollo program, we embark on this journey for all humanity. Unlike Apollo, we will be going to stay … We seek the capacity for people to work, learn, operate, and sustainably live beyond Earth for extended periods of time. Any journey to Mars will take many months each way and early return is not an option."

A self-portrait taken by NASA's *Curiosity* Mars rover

According to NASA's plans, early steps will include experiments aboard the International Space Station to determine how crews can live for long periods of time in space. In particular, NASA will focus on the effects of space radiation on health, which has long been the fear of putting astronauts on long space trips. In order to address this, new technologies will need to be developed in order to limit the amount of space radiation that crew members are exposed to during long missions.

Later steps will include sending crews to orbit the moon, and then to land on the moon in order to build colonies using modular designs and 3D printing. Other tasks will include sending cargo and supplies to Mars during unmanned missions. An important part of this is NASA's Mars probes, which have been exploring Mars for approximately forty years. These probes will continue to send important information about the red planet back to Earth and will enable scientists to begin to study the Martian atmosphere and the possibility of human life on Mars. Perhaps most exciting, NASA is working on plans to develop more powerful spacecraft that use solar electric energy to propel them through space. Mars is an average of 140 million miles (225 million km) from Earth, depending on the positions of the planets, and it is estimated that it would take six months to arrive at Mars from Earth. One of the biggest issues that NASA will need to address is how to power a spacecraft for such a long period of time while also building a spacecraft that is aerodynamically and physically reliable and safe, not to mention the cost of developing such new technology. Experts believe the lowest estimate comes in around $76 million. Overcoming these obstacles is not an easy feat, although private companies such as SpaceX have already voiced ways of addressing these problems.

SpaceX has announced that its *Dragon* capsule would be the right spacecraft for the mission. The *Dragon* made history when it docked with the International Space Station in 2012 as the first commercially-built spacecraft to do so. In April 2016, SpaceX announced that it is planning for a 2018 launch using the *Dragon* and Falcon Heavy launchers for an unmanned mission to Mars. Although NASA is not part of the planning, the governmental agency will be providing technical support.

The *Red Dragon*, a new spacecraft announced in September 2016, would be used for this unmanned mission to Mars. It has four thruster pods mounted on its sides to propel the craft into space. It also has two SuperDraco engines mounted to each thruster pod. These engines use SpaceX technology to provide propellant—a mixture of monomethylhydrazine fuel and dinitrogen tetroxide oxidizer. These propellants are storable and can be restarted multiple times, allowing for different stages of propulsion. The SuperDraco engine is one of the most powerful engines ever built. The planned mission would have the Red Dragon voyage to Mars with everything it needed to gather samples on Mars and return, including a Mars Ascent Vehicle and an Earth Return Vehicle. NASA has promised to provide technical support in exchange for the data SpaceX accumulates from this mission.

Musk has stated in the past that a separate vehicle, a *Mars Colonial Transporter* (*MCT*), would be about "100 times the size of an SUV" in order to transport 100 people at once to Mars. Tom Mueller, the head of engine development at SpaceX, has stated that nine engines would be needed to support such a large spacecraft with so many people aboard. In June 2016, Musk gave out further information about development of the mission when he stated that the first *Mars Colonial Transporter* flight was planned for a 2022 launch without passengers. The first manned *MCT* mission is planned for 2024. This is earlier than the planned Mars missions by NASA.

As for practical details about the trip, Musk has stated that a ticket to Mars would cost on the order of $500,000 dollars and only ten people would complete the first voyage.

NASA, meanwhile, is also already in the active stages of their plan for a 2030 manned Mars mission. The first component of NASA's Mars mission was launched successfully on December 5, 2014. The *Orion* Multi-Purpose

Crew Vehicle (*Orion* MPCV) spent over four hours in outer space on a test flight before landing in the Pacific Ocean. It weighs about 25 tons (23 t), which is 7.7 tons (7 t less than the *Apollo* command and service module. The crew module, however, is larger than the *Apollo* cabin at nearly 9.9 tons (9 t) compared to *Apollo*'s 6.6 tons (6 t). Like SpaceX's *Dragon* spacecraft, the *Orion* MPCV uses hypergolic propellants, in which a fuel and an oxider spontaneously ignite when they come into contact with one another. The *Orion* MPCV is based on *Apollo*'s design, in which there is a command module where the crew stays and a service module that holds the spacecraft's propulsion system. The command module, designed by Lockheed Martin would hold four to six crew members. However, the technology on the *Orion* MPCV is much more advanced, and it is designed for long periods of space travel of at least six months. The *Orion* MPCV is also designed to be upgradable as new technologies are developed. Other developments include the use of a "glass cockpit" as used in advanced aircraft, which shows data displays on large LCD screens, and auto-piloting features, including computer-led auto-docking. Unlike SpaceX spacecraft, the *Orion* MPCV will be recovered after water landings only. During launch, the *Orion* MPCV will use the Launch Escape System (LES) and a protective cover made of fiberglass, making it ten times safer during the critical periods of launching and reentry than the previous reusable NASA Space Shuttle.

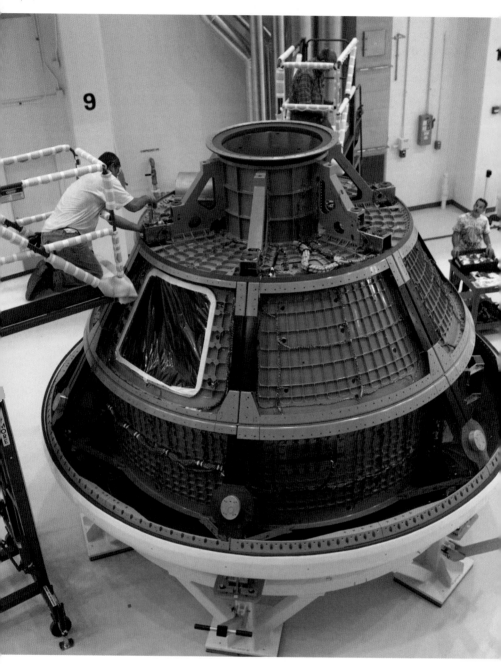

An *Orion* test vehicle is constructed at NASA in 2012.

Telescopes, Probes, Spacecraft, and the Future of Space Exploration

The LES aborts the mission during launch if the onboard computer detects a problem, separating the crew from the faulty spacecraft with a rocket-motored abort vehicle. The command module of the MPCV will be reusable after flight.

The first Exploration Mission will take place on September 30, 2018, at the Kennedy Space Center. The *Orion* MPCV will be launched from the new Space Launch System, which is one of the most powerful rockets ever built, and will spend three weeks in space, including six days in orbit around the moon. The next planned launch for the *Orion* MPCV will be in 2023, although NASA officials have admitted to an internal goal they hope to reach by 2021.

That's not the only exciting project NASA is working on. The agency is also developing the James Webb Space Telescope (JWST), which is scheduled for launch in October, 2018. The JWST is a successor to the famous Hubble Telescope and is the most advanced telescope of its kind. Named after NASA administrator James E. Webb, an integral part of the Apollo program, this telescope was first planned in 1996 and is a collaboration between NASA, the United States space agency, the European Space Agency, and the Canadian Space Agency.

The JWST is expected to be about half the size of the Hubble Telescope, although its 21-foot (6.5 m) primary mirror will have a **collecting area** five times as large as that telescope. It has near-perfect resolution and can see from near-infrared to mid-infrared. It will also notably have a sun shield to protect instrumentation from solar heat. The mirror is too large to launchso it is made up of eighteen different beryllium segments which will "unfold" after launch. Secondary and tertiary mirrors help to correct any image aberration and another fast-steering mirror will help to stabilize the image.

The mirrors will be mounted on the Integrated Science Instrument Module (ISIM), which provides power, steering, and stability, as well as additional guidance and instrumentation. The ISIM holds a Near Infrared Camera (NIRCam), a Near Infrared Spectrograph (NIRSpec), a Mid-Infrared Instrument (MIRI), and a Fine Guidance Sensor (FGS). The FGS navigates the spacecraft in a controlled way through space.

A project of this magnitude is likely to have some setbacks, and the JWST has had its share of these. Originally planned for 2011, the JWST launch has been pushed back seven years largely due to budget cutbacks. In 2011, the US House of Representatives voted to halt funding on the project, although three billion dollars had already been spent in its development. This vote did not go through, however, and funding was restored to eight billion dollars. Full-scale models of the telescope have been on display around the world since 2005 in order to increase public knowledge of and support for the project.

NASA has four primary goals for the JWTS mission. First, it hopes to use the telescope to detect the light of the first stars and galaxies after the big bang. Finding light can help scientists learn about the big bang and the environment of the early universe. Second, NASA hopes to use the telescope to learn more about how galaxies form and evolve. This could teach us more about the evolution of our universe and provide useful information about the lifecycle of our own galaxy, the Milky Way. Third and fourth, NASA scientists hope to study the formation of stars and planetary systems. All of these goals will help NASA to better understand the origin of life itself from its origins in the big bang.

Universities and academics are also making exciting new discoveries based on new technologies. In turn, these discoveries are powering new and more ambitious missions into space. At the Laser Interferometer Gravitational-Wave Observatory (LIGO) at Caltech, experiments are being conducted that have, for the first time ever, detected gravitational waves. Gravitational waves were first predicted by Albert Einstein at the beginning of the twentieth century but were ignored for over fifty years as an implausible theory. Then, in 1974, proof came. Astronomers at the Arecibo Radio Observatory in Puerto Rico discovered a binary pulsar, which is two dense stars orbiting around one another. They began to observe the system in the hopes of confirming

The Laser Interferometer Gravitational-Wave Observatory (LIGO)

Telescopes, Probes, Spacecraft, and the Future of Space Exploration

Einstein's theory. And they did. In fact, the system emulated Einstein's predictions so well that, although they did not actually observe gravitational waves themselves, they were sure that they existed. The astronomers, Russell Hulse and Joseph Taylor, received the Nobel Prize in Physics for their discovery.

So what are gravitational waves and why is this discovery so exciting? According to Einstein's theory of general relativity, very large and accelerating objects disturb the fabric of space-time, sending ripples or waves of this distorted space outward. A good way of imagining this is by thinking of the ripples of waves that move outward when you throw a pebble into a pond. These ripples would travel at the speed of light and, if we were able to intercept and detect them, they would give us a lot of information about the events that caused them and even about gravity itself (Much of gravity is still a mystery to scientists who study very large-scale objects, like astronomers, and those who study very small-scale objects, like molecular physicists). Detecting these gravitational waves would also be additional confirmation that Einstein's theories (and some of his most controversial theories) were indeed correct.

Astronomers have long been using radio telescopes to try to detect pulsar radio emissions to confirm the existence of gravitational waves. But, like in 1974, they never actually detected them, although mathematically they proved that they existed.

That is, until 2015. On September 14, 2015, scientists at LIGO used a powerful new device to sense distortions in space-time. The gravitational waves that they sensed came from two black holes colliding over 1.3 million light years away. This was no easy task, as the distortion was more than thousands of times smaller than the nucleus of an atom.

The device scientists used, an interferometer, is a new and extremely complex machine that is used on Earth to better understand the universe around us. LIGO actually consists of two interferometers, with 2.5-mile (4 km) long arms that are arranged in the shape of an L. Like telescopes, interferometers use mirrors to merge sources of light. However, the interferometer gets its name because it makes patterns of light, called an "**interference pattern**," that contain information that scientists can then study about the source of the light. The strength of this kind of machine is that it can measure tiny distances, thousandths of times smaller than a subatomic particle.

First, a laser beam is sent through a mirror that splits the light into two different beams. One beam travels straight down the path of one arm of the interferometer, while the other beam is reflected at a 90-degree angle down the other arm of the machine. At the end of each arm, a mirror reflects the beams of light back until they merge again

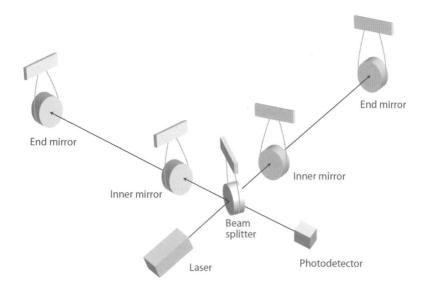

This diagram shows how light travels down the two arms of the interferometer.

at the start. Because of the properties of light, if the two beams travel the exact same distance, meaning that the arms of the interferometer are the exact same length, then the **photodetector** detects nothing at all. However, if one beam travels faster than the other, meaning that the distance of one of the arms has changed, then one beam of light hits first, which shows an "interference pattern" that changes the light intensity. When the gravitational waves were detected in September 2015, this registered as a blip of light.

What this means is, most simply, the interferometer detected a gravitational wave, which distorted space-time in such a way that the length of one arm of the machine became almost imperceptibly smaller than the other arm of the machine, although both were built to be equal. This means that as gravitational waves pass among us, space is contracting and expanding all around us!

Following this exciting discovery, astronomers claimed that this was opening a "new era" and a "new field of astrophysics." Why? Because almost every single telescope that we have detects X-rays, gamma-rays, visible light, and radio waves. But there are many other ways to observe the universe, although we have not often been able to detect them. Detecting gravitational waves is another way of examining the universe that has not yet been used on a grand level. Imagine how much information is out there if we began to build more and more complex tools, including new kinds of "telescopes," in order to examine this invisible aspect of our world?

The promise of gravitational waves is exciting because it will allow scientists to study objects that do not radiate any form of light, particularly black holes, dark matter, and dark energy. Black holes are called "black" because no light can escape from them. Astronomers cannot actually "see" them using the most advanced telescopes but can detect them by the way they distort light around them.

Mars One Astronauts

Who are the people who would volunteer for a one-way mission to Mars? Apparently, they come from a wide range of backgrounds and hope to take part in a historic first mission to Mars for many reasons—from wanting to advance science to an insatiable thirst for adventure.

Mars One selected one hundred candidates for its first mission to Mars, the controversial project scheduled for 2026. Of these one hundred candidates, only four will be selected for the final mission. Fifty men and fifty women made it to the third round of selection, and they come from all around the world. The next rounds of selection will focus on creating teams that would work well together during the high-stress atmosphere of a first mission to Mars. Over two hundred thousand candidates initially applied.

Joseph Roche, selected as a Mars One astronaut, wrote, "I volunteered for the Mars One program because my research areas include astrophysics and the role of science in society. I am passionate about pushing the boundaries of scientific endeavor and that is why the ambitiousness of the Mars One plan appealed to me." However, he criticized the Mars One project and said that people need to focus on more viable options after experiencing the selection process, which he said was not rigorous enough for such an ambitious project.

According to science writer Calla Colfield:

> LIGO can see things that no other observatory can, and that's a big reason why people are calling this the beginning of a new era of astrophysics. LIGO will spot many other objects, including exploding stars (supernovas) and mergers between neutron stars, or the nuggets of leftover star explosions that are just slightly not dense enough to become black holes.
>
> But there will also be great discoveries when LIGO works with light-based telescopes and observatories. Those instruments can "see" the universe, and LIGO can "hear" it—and they're best when used together, just as movies are best when they are both seen and heard or food is best when both tasted and smelled. "Multimessenger astronomy" refers to the combination of different kinds of astronomical information, such as light and gravitational waves. It's a new chapter in astrophysics, and LIGO has just given it a big boost.

Current teams are working on developing other gravitational-wave detectors in Italy, Japan, and India. Scientists and engineers are also developing plans for space-based gravitational-wave detectors that would be launched into space like our current telescopes. Working in conjunction with telescopes that "see" light, these new machines promise to open up our universe even further with consequences that are still unknown.

We have come a long way from the first telescope that Galileo used, a simple tube with lenses affixed on both ends, to stare up at the sky and start an astronomical revolution. Today, scientists use enormous telescopes that use a combination of lenses and mirrors, as well as radio telescopes, high-pixel cameras, spectrographs, inferometers, and new kinds of instruments to understand our universe. We have explored our skies even farther, through probes and manned missions to areas far beyond our Earth. And we will keep exploring, either on Earth or far beyond—either as brief visitors, or to stay. The future holds many exciting revelations for our exploration of space.

Glossary

aperture The opening through which light passes on an optical instrument, especially a camera.

array An arrangement or related elements or objects; in astronomy, a grouping of linked telescopes.

chromatic aberration Caused by the refraction of different waves of light, this causes a blurry image.

collecting area The amount of area a telescope has to collect electromagnetic radiation.

concave Curving inward like the interior of a sphere.

convex Curving outward like the exterior of a sphere.

cosmic microwave background radiation (CMB) Thermal radiation left over from the big bang.

electromagnetic spectrum The range of wavelengths over which electromagnetic radiation, including visible light, radio waves, gamma rays, and X-rays, extends.

exposure The act of exposing photographic film to light.

fiscal Of or relating to government revenue, especially taxes.

general relativity The theory of gravitation proposed by Albert Einstein in 1915, which states that all observers, regardless of their state of motion, will observe the same laws of physics.

heliocentric A system in which the sun is at the center.

infrared Part of the electromagnetic spectrum that is invisible to the human eye and has longer wavelengths than visible light.

interference pattern The pattern that develops when two or more waves of light interfere with one another.

orbital Relating to the curved path an object takes around a star, planet, or moon, which is held in place by gravity.

parabolic Like a U shape.

photodetector A device that detects light through detecting electrical effects of individual photons.

reflecting When a surface throws back light without absorbing it.

refracting When light changes its angle after entering into air, water, glass, etc.

satellite A man-made object or celestial body orbiting around a planet or moon.

spectrographs A device for photographing spectra, or different wavelengths of light.

suborbital A trajectory that does not complete a full orbit around a celestial body, such as the Earth.

Further Information

Books

Basher, Simon. *Basher Basics: Space Exploration*. New York: Kingfisher, 2013.

Dickinson, Terence. *Hubble's Universe: Greatest Discoveries and Latest Images*. Ontario, Canada: Firefly Books, 2014.

Sagan, Carl. *Cosmos*. New York: Ballantine Books, 2013.

Stott, Carole. *DK Eyewitness Books: Space Exploration*. New York: DK Kids, 2014.

Websites

The Apollo Missions
http://www.nasa.gov/mission_pages/apollo/missions
This NASA website explores all of the Apollo missions and includes photos, featured stories, and technical specifications for the Apollo spacecraft.

Laser Interferometer Gravitational-Wave Observatory (LIGO)

https://www.ligo.caltech.edu

Explore LIGO's website, where they provide information about their search for and confirmation of gravitational waves and more technical descriptions of their interferometers.

Space X

http://www.spacex.com

The SpaceX website offers technical specifications for its spacecraft and news about past and current missions.

Organizations and Museums

Hayden Planetarium

79 Central Park West

New York, NY 10024

(212) 769-5100

http://www.amnh.org/our-research/hayden-planetarium

Kennedy Space Center Visitor Complex

SR 405

Titusville, FL 32899

(321) 452-2121

https://www.kennedyspacecenter.com

Bibliography

"About LIGO: Laser Interferometer Gravitational-Wave Observatory." LIGO. Accessed June 27, 2016. https://www.ligo.caltech.edu.

Cox, Lauren. "Who Invented the Telescope?" *Space. com*. July 13, 2013. http://www.space.com/21950-who-invented-the-telescope.html.

"Dragon." *SpaceX*. Accessed June 27, 2016. http://www.spacex.com/dragon.

"Fact Sheets: NASA Langley Research Center's Contributions to the Apollo Program." *NASA*. Accessed June 27, 2016. http://www.nasa.gov/centers/langley/news/factsheets/Apollo.html.

"Overview: The Dark Energy Survey." *The Dark Energy Survey*. Accessed June 27, 2016. http://www.darkenergysurvey.org/the-des-project/overview.

Panek, Richard. "Dark Energy: The Biggest Mystery of
the Universe." *Smithsonian Magazine*, April 2010.
http://www.smithsonianmag.com/science-nature/
dark-energy-the-biggest-mystery-in-the-universe-
9482130/?all.

Penzias, Arno. "The Origin of Elements." Nobel Prize.org.
December 8, 1978. http://www.nobelprize.org/nobel_
prizes/physics/laureates/1978/penzias-lecture.pdf.

Rayl, A.J.S. "NASA Engineers and Scientists-Transforming
Dreams into Reality." *NASA Magazine*. Accessed
June 27, 2016. http://www.nasa.gov/50th/50th_
magazine/scientists.html.

"Virgin Galactic's SpaceShipTwo Mothership Makes
Maiden Flight." Space Fellowship. December 21,
2008. http://spacefellowship.com/news/art7772/virgin-
galactic-039-s-spaceshiptwo-mothership-makes-
maiden-flight.html.

"What's Next for NASA?" NASA. July 1, 2011. http://www.
nasa.gov/about/whats_next.html.

Young, Monica. "Mapping Dark Matter." *Sky and
Telescope*. May 7, 2015. http://www.skyandtelescope.
com/astronomy-news/mapping-dark-matter-05071532.

Index

About the Author

Elizabeth Schmermund is a writer, scholar, and editor. While her days are mostly filled with literature—and not necessarily astronomical study—she has always had a great curiosity for astronomy and physics. At one time, she planned to graduate with a degree in astronomy and even had the opportunity to conduct research at Kitt Peak in Arizona and the Mauna Kea Observatories on the Big Island of Hawaii. Today, she has a telescope and loves staring out at the planets and stars with her husband and her young son. She credits Carl Sagan with initiating her love of astronomy at a young age.